REVIVED

Revived

A STUDY OF
PSALM 85

Gwendolyn Harmon

Learning Ladyhood Press

Contents

Foreword   1

1   The Foundation of Revival   2

2   The Need for Revival   9

3   Steps of Revival: Hear Him   16

4   Steps of Revival: Turn   22

5   Results of Revival   28

Foreword

We often speak of revival in a collective sense: our nation needs revival, our churches need revival, our whole world needs revival—and that is certainly true. But while God's message to the nation of Israel called them to a national return to God, that collective call necessarily encompassed the individual hearts of His children.

Psalm 85 is often called the "revival psalm," because it gives us an honest but encouraging glimpse into how revival works. So, dear reader, let's take a walk together through this psalm and drink in what God says about revival.

1

The Foundation of Revival

*"Lord, Thou hast been favourable unto Thy land:
Thou hast brought back the captivity of Jacob. Thou
hast forgiven the iniquity of Thy people, Thou hast
covered all their sin. Selah.*

*Thou hast taken away all Thy wrath: Thou hast
turned Thyself from the fierceness of Thine anger."*
(vv.1-3)

I do not know exactly when this psalm was written, but
the reference to God being favorable to His land and bring-
ing back the *captivity* of Jacob gives us a clue. This psalm was
likely written after the years of exile, possibly during the time
of Ezra and Nehemiah.

This also fits with the theme of revival, since those who returned from the exile quickly fell back into their old habits of serving self instead of God. The need for revival can be seen fairly early in the accounts of the Jewish people's return to the land.

But although these verses are valuable for helping us understand the historical context of the psalm, they should also be verses that resonate with our hearts today.

"Lord, Thou hast been favourable unto Thy land..."

Take a moment and consider: has God been favorable to you? That word, favorable, in the Hebrew means "to be pleased with" and is specifically used regarding the satisfaction of a debt. Has God satisfied your debt?

You and I each have a debt we can never pay: the debt of our sin. Romans 3:23 tells us that,

"All have sinned, and come short of the glory of God."

The nation of Israel had the sacrificial system, but the book of Hebrews makes it clear that animal sacrifices were simply not sufficient—and that they were never designed to be.

The debt of sin can never be washed away by anything you or I could do. Consider the following:

"For the law having a shadow of good things to come, and not the very image of the things, can never with those sacrifices which they offered year by year continually make the comers thereunto perfect. For then would they not have ceased to be offered? because that the worshippers once purged should have had no more conscience of sins. But in those sacrifices there is a remembrance again made of sins every year. For it is not possible that the blood of bulls and of goats should take away sins." (Hebrews 10:1-4)

"For by grace are ye saved through faith; and that not of yourselves: it is the gift of God: Not of works, lest any man should boast." (Ephesians 2:8-9)

2 Corinthians 5:21 tells us that Christ took on our unpayable debt of sin, giving us His righteousness in exchange:

"For He hath made Him to be sin for us, who knew no sin; that we might be made the righteousness of God in Him."

Regardless of whatever else is happening in your life, if you are saved, you can truly say that God has bestowed His favor upon you! But there are many facets of salvation for which the saved in Christ can (and should) be thankful.

Thou hast brought back the captivity of Jacob. Thou hast forgiven the iniquity of Thy people, Thou hast covered all their sin.

Has God brought back the captivity of your soul? Romans 7 describes the bondage of sin and our helplessness to free ourselves. Then, in the very first verse of Romans 8 we find this awe-inspiring truth:

"There is therefore now no condemnation to them which are in Christ Jesus, who walk not after the flesh, but after the Spirit."

As Jesus said to the believing Jews in John 8:32, *"And ye shall know the truth, and the truth shall make you free."* And just a few verses later, Jesus adds, *"If the Son therefore shall make you free, ye shall be free indeed." (v.36)*

Romans 6:18 quite simply states: *"Being then made free from sin, ye became the servants of righteousness"* and Romans 6:22 tells us, *"But now being made free from sin, and become servants to God, ye have your fruit unto holiness, and the end everlasting life."*

We are freed from sin, not to sin more (see Romans 6:1-2), but rather, to reflect the righteousness of Christ through our lives. Matthew 5:16 gives us a picture of this:

"Let your light so shine before men, that they may see your good works, and glorify your Father which is in heaven."

Thou hast taken away all Thy wrath: Thou hast turned Thyself from the fierceness of Thine anger.

Has God's wrath been turned away from you? Romans 5:9 says,

"Much more then, being now justified by His blood, we shall be saved from wrath through Him."

And 1 Thessalonians 1:10 says that Jesus Christ delivers us from the wrath to come. In 1 Thessalonians we also read this blessed truth wrapped in an admonition:

"But let us, who are of the day, be sober, putting on the breastplate of faith and love; and for an helmet, the hope of salvation. For God hath not appointed us to wrath, but to obtain salvation by our Lord Jesus Christ, Who died for us, that, whether we wake or sleep, we should live together with Him." (5:8-10)

Instead of the wrath of God, we who have received Christ's payment for our sins are now guaranteed His love. Romans 8 beautifully illustrates this:

"Who shall separate us from the love of Christ? shall tribulation, or distress, or persecution, or famine, or nakedness, or peril, or sword? As it is written, For Thy sake we are killed all the day long; we are accounted as sheep for the slaughter. Nay in all these things we are more than conquerors through Him that loved us.

For I am persuaded, that neither death, nor life, nor angels, nor principalities, nor powers, nor things present, nor things to come, Nor height, nor depth, nor any other creature, shall be able to separate us from the love of God, which is in Christ Jesus our Lord." (vv. 35-39)

Are you in Christ today? Have you traded the terror of God's just wrath for the fulness of His perfect love? If so, these first few verses of Psalm 85 should be joyously familiar to you.

Putting it into Practice:

The starting place for revival is salvation. We cannot revive that which was never alive. As Romans 3:23 tells us, *"all have sinned, and come short of the glory of God."*

We have all broken the law of God, we are all in need of His forgiveness. The sacrifice of Jesus Christ on the cross provided us with a choice:

"For the wages of sin is death; but the gift of God is eternal life through Jesus Christ our Lord." Romans 6:23

We can choose eternal death or eternal life—but remember, the choice for eternal life is a choice we must deliberately make. Eternal life is not our default.

Have you admitted your sin to God and accepted the gift of salvation already purchased for you? If so, rejoice in God's salvation! For the saved in Christ, the need for revival often comes when we forget to rejoice in the salvation and mercy of God.

"Restore unto me the joy of Thy salvation; and uphold me with Thy free Spirit." Psalm 51:12

2

The Need for Revival

*"Turn us, O God of our salvation, and cause
Thine anger toward us to cease. Wilt Thou be angry
with us for ever? Wilt Thou draw out Thine anger
to all generations? Wilt Thou not revive us again:
that Thy people may rejoice in Thee? Shew us Thy
mercy, O Lord, and grant us Thy salvation."*
Psalm 85:4-7

Despite the salvation God has already given to us: the forgiveness already extended, the pardon already granted, you
and I are not yet made perfect. We are still sinners—sinners
saved by grace—but sinners nevertheless.

1 John addresses this when He writes to fellow believers:

"If we say that we have no sin, we deceive ourselves, and the truth is not in us." (1:8)

For us to think or act as if Christ's forgiveness of our sins has made us suddenly incapable of sinning is not just foolish: it is a deception. And yet, in a subtle way, we often fall into that very deception by simple neglect of our relationship with God. We get comfortable, and stop actively trying to walk in the Spirit, relying instead on habit, emotions, or routine.

Cause Thine anger toward us to cease...

Notice that the psalmist pleads with God for the turning away of His anger. In the books of Ezra, Nehemiah and the "minor" prophets who wrote at the time of the return to the land, we see that the people quickly turned away from following the Lord.

Some disobeyed God's commands and married foreign wives. They eventually allowed their pagan culture to define their homes and families. Others grew discouraged and gave up the work of rebuilding the temple, while some simply became too absorbed in their own daily lives to obey God's call to rebuild.

You and I can easily walk right into the same kinds of traps as the post-exile Israelites. We are constantly bombarded by worldly influences, and the pressure to allow the culture around us to push God out of our homes, our minds, and our daily lives is stronger than we tend to realize. The drift away from God can happen without our even noticing.

It is important to remember that while the need for revival does sometimes result from a believer rebelliously clinging to blatant, obvious sin, it more often results from the slow backward slipping of neglect.

This is not what God wants for His children. The Christian life is not one of apathy, but of a holy urgency. Consider Paul, who said,

"Brethren, I count not myself to have apprehended: but this one thing I do, forgetting those things which are behind, and reaching forth unto those things which are before, I press toward the mark for the high calling of God in Christ Jesus." Philippians 3:13-14

That word "*press*" means to pursue, to follow after. It is also used in reference to Paul's persecution of believers *(Acts 22:4, 22:7).*

Just as he had chased the believers down, wanting to take them captive and make them submit to what *he* thought was the true worship of God, so now he drove *himself* on. He took his thoughts and imaginations captive *(2 Corinthians 10:5)* and forced his old nature to submit to the will of God.

Paul met Christ while relentlessly pursuing believers, and his life's work became instead the relentless pursuit of holiness and a deeper knowledge of God.

Maintaining Peace

As mentioned in the last chapter, we who have trusted Christ's finished work as payment for our sins have traded the wrath of God for a loving relationship with Him. In Christ we have true peace with God, but that peace doesn't mean we are to be passive.

We are to be active in the fight against the temptations thrown at us by the world, the flesh, and the Devil. Here are just a couple passages that illustrate the urgency and vigilance the Christian life requires:

"Finally, my brethren, be strong in the Lord, and in the power of His might. Put on the whole armor of God, that ye may be able to stand against the wiles of the devil. For we wrestle not against flesh and blood, but against principalities, against powers, against the rulers of the darkness of this world, against spiritual wickedness in high places. Wherefore take unto you the whole armor of God, that ye may be able to withstand in the evil day, and having done all, to stand." (Ephesians 6:10-13)

"Know ye not that they which run in a race run all, but one receiveth the prize? So run, that ye may obtain. And every man that striveth for the mastery is temperate in all things. Now, they do it to obtain a corruptible crown; but we an incorruptible. I therefore so run, not as uncertainly; so fight I, not as one that beateth the air: But I keep under my body, and bring it into subjection: lest that by any means, when I have preached to others, I myself should be a castaway." (1 Corinthians 9:24-27)

Peace at Work

The same Jesus who said, *"Peace I leave with you, My peace I give unto you" (John 14:27)* also commanded,

"Go ye therefore, and teach all nations, baptizing them in the name of the Father, and of the Son, and of the Holy Ghost: Teaching them to observe all things whatsoever I have commanded you: and, lo, I am with you alway, even unto the end of the world. Amen." (Matthew 28:19-20)

The peace of God is actually found as we press forward in obedience to God, empowered by His Spirit. Galatians gives us a glimpse of what Spirit-led living looks like:

"But the fruit of the Spirit is love, joy, peace, longsuffering, gentleness, goodness, faith, Meekness, temperance: against such there is no law." (Galatians 5:22-23)

All this results from that same pressing forward of which Paul spoke. The Spirit does not indwell us to enable lethargy, but action.

If we would enjoy the fruit of longsuffering in our lives, we must, through the Spirit's power, face a situation in which we must suffer long. If we would be gentle or good, we must face the temptation to harshness or wickedness, and conquer through the power of the Holy Spirit.

The fruit of the Spirit is remarkable because it is contrary to our natural inclinations. It only comes when we choose to say yes to God, and no to sin. It is a nine-part description of what it looks like to live out the words of Galatians 5:16,

"This I say then, Walk in the Spirit, and ye shall not fulfil the lust of the flesh."

Putting it into Practice:

Are you in need of revival today? Has the world crept into your life, your thinking, your heart? Are you lacking the fruit of the Spirit? You never can bring forth that fruit on your own.

Revival is not the rebuilding of spiritual life by our own effort, but rather a surrender to the *Spirit's* rebuilding work. Give all to God, hold back nothing from Him. Yield to the promptings of the Holy Spirit, and you will find that revival is not so far away as it seemed.

"If we live in the Spirit, let us also walk in the Spirit." Galatians 5:25

3

Steps of Revival: Hear Him

"I will hear what God the Lord will speak: for He will speak peace unto His people, and to His saints: but let them not turn again to folly."
Psalm 85:8

In the last chapter, we saw the need for revival, and how it often stems from neglect of our relationship with God. We may desire revival, as the psalmist did, crying out to God, *"Wilt Thou not revive us again: that Thy people may rejoice in Thee?" (Psalm 85:6)*

And yet, while we may recognize the need for revival, we often think it is something far off, beyond our reach unless God decides to do some large-scale miracle.

But revival is powerfully personal, and happens heart by heart. If you study out the history of large-scale revivals such as the Welsh Revival or the Great Awakening, you will see that that they rose and fell upon the responses of individual hearts to the truths presented.

But if revival is possible for the individual, the question becomes, *How?*

The key is found in verse 8 of Psalm 85: *"I will hear what God the Lord will speak: for He will speak peace unto His people, and to His saints: but let them not turn again to folly."*

Notice the first step: *"I will hear what God the Lord will speak."* If you want to be revived, you have to *hear* what God says. This has two aspects:

Hearing the Word of God

One sure way to hear what God says is to read what He has *already* said to us in His Word. Time spent in the Bible, reading, studying, and pondering is never wasted. It is during those times that the Holy Spirit speaks to us, pointing out a verse or striking a truth home to our hearts.

As Paul wrote to Timothy in 2 Timothy 2:15, *"Study to shew thyself approved unto God, a workman that needeth not to be ashamed, rightly dividing the Word of truth."*

Psalm 119 is an excellent passage to read if you want to know what a Christian's relationship with the Word of God should be. Here are just a few verses that get us started in the right direction:

"Thy word have I hid in mine heart, that I might not sin against Thee." (v.11)

"The law of Thy mouth is better unto me than thousands of gold and silver." (v.72)

"Unless Thy law had been my delights, I should then have perished in mine affliction."(v.92)

"O how love I Thy law! It is my meditation all the day." (v.97)

"How sweet are Thy words unto my taste! Yea, sweeter than honey to my mouth!" (v.103)

"Thy word is a lamp unto my feet, and a light unto my path." (v.105)

"Great peace have they which love Thy law: and nothing shall offend them." (v.165)

It can be difficult to carve out large chunks of time for Bible study, but it is always worth the effort! And passages committed to memory can be carried around in one's heart and mind, to be pondered on or reveled in throughout the day.

This is what is meant when the word "meditation" is used. We are to keep God's Word with us all day long, thinking about it, turning it over in our minds and delighting in its truth.

God's Word not only helps us fight temptation and grow closer to God, but also builds our faith: Romans 10:17 says,

"So then faith cometh by hearing, and hearing by the Word of God."

The context of this verse is primarily about salvation, but the principle holds true for the believer as well. Our faith is built when we know God's Word and recognize how it applies to our lives. When we know what God has promised, and trust God to fulfil those promises, our faith is strengthened.

When we read a narrative passage and realize it has parallels to a situation we are facing, we see the character of God on display and are equipped to recognize it in our own situation as well, and by that, our faith is strengthened.

Hearing the Spirit of God

The other aspect of hearing what God has to say is listening to the Holy Spirit.

We often treat the Holy Spirit like something vague and intangible. But the Holy Spirit isn't just a force or energy: He is a Person, fully equal and fully unified with God the Father and Jesus, God the Son. If you have trusted Christ as your Savior, you have *God Himself living in you.*

And why does God Himself choose to indwell believers? Here's what Jesus said the Holy Spirit would do for us:

"But the Comforter, which is the Holy Ghost, whom the Father will send in My name, He shall teach you all things, and bring all things to your remembrance, whatsoever I have said unto you." John 14:26

Even when we do not have a Bible in front of our eyes, the Holy Spirit can bring to remembrance the things we have read and memorized from God's Word. We have already looked at Psalm 119:11, which touches on this truth:

"Thy Word have I hid in mine heart, that I might not sin against Thee."

The Holy Spirit uses the Word of God to teach us, to comfort us, and to convict our hearts of sin.

Putting it into Practice

Neglect of the Bible and neglect of prayer allow the clamor of the world to drown out the Spirit's voice. If you want revival, you must be ready *and* willing to hear what God has to say to you.

"Blessed are they that hear the word of God, and keep it." Luke 11:28

4

Steps of Revival: Turn

"I will hear what God the Lord will speak: for He will speak peace unto His saints: but let them not turn again to folly." (v.8)

After pleading for revival, our psalmist makes a statement that paints a picture for us of what true heart-deep revival looks like.

As we saw in the last chapter, revival begins with a willingness to hear what God has to say. This requires time, effort, and a humility before the Lord.

We often reject revival simply by responding in pride to the Holy Spirit's promptings. But when we are willing to give up our pride and yield to what God has to say about our lives, our hearts, and our sin, then true revival begins.

Hearing is crucial, but at the same time, there is more involved in revival than the mere hearing of truth. James says,

"But be ye doers of the Word, and not hearers only, deceiving your own selves." 1:22

Pride may give assent to the truth, but falls short of obedience. The prideful Christian takes the Word of God and says intellectually, "That's right. I agree with that," then goes away and does his or her own thing, assuming that the truth was for some other person. But God's Word always leads the hearer to some kind of action.

You and I are not perfect. There will always be something God wants us to change, and that is where the second step of revival comes in. We need to *turn*. Isaiah puts it this way:

"Let the wicked forsake his way, and the unrighteous man his thoughts: and let him return unto the Lord, and He will have mercy upon him; and to our God, for He will abundantly pardon." (55:7)

A renewed walk with God means a renewed walk *away* from those things that do not please Him. Whether it's blatant sin others might easily recognize, or something more subtle, saying "yes" to God requires saying "no" to sin.

James chapter 2 repeats the statement that *"faith without works is dead." (v.20, 26)*

And what is revival but the renewing of our faith? By grace we are saved, through faith, and it is that same faith by which we walk with God, empowered by His grace. Colossians 2:6 tells us,

"As ye have therefore received Christ Jesus the Lord, so walk ye in Him."

James again gives us this helpful statement: *"Yea, a man may say, Thou hast faith, and I have works: shew me thy faith without thy works, and I will shew thee my faith by my works." (2:18)*

Faith leads us to action, and *"faith cometh by hearing, and hearing by the Word of God" (Romans 10:17).*

Perhaps this is why Christ emphasizes works in His letter to the church in Ephesus in the book of Revelation:

"I know thy works, and thy labour, and thy patience, and how thou canst not bear them which are evil: and thou hast tried them which say they are apostles, and are not, and hast found them liars: and hast borne, and hast patience, and for My name's sake hast laboured, and hast not fainted. Nevertheless I have somewhat against thee, because thou hast left thy first love. Remember therefore from whence thou art fallen, and repent, and do the first works..." (2:2-5a)

At first, you might read all the good works this church had done and think, "Why would *this* church need revival?" But notice what was missing in their actions: their *"first love."* In the abundance of their working for God, the work itself had become their focus, eclipsing love for God. Christ tells this active but empty church to *"Remember from whence thou art fallen."*

J. I. Packer once said,

> "Revival always includes a profound awareness of one's own sinfulness, leading to deep repentance and heartfelt embrace of the glorified, loving, pardoning Christ."*

For the church at Ephesus in ancient times as well as for you and me today, the path to repentance starts with the Holy Spirit's conviction. Sometimes, we need to be reminded of how fresh and sweet our walk with God used to be. We need to realize what's missing.

But once we feel how far we have drifted from the real, vibrant, soul-satisfying relationship with God, then what are we to do?

Repent. That word literally means to think differently, or reconsider. We need to change our minds about how we are living, about how we have been responding to the Holy

Spirit. This change of mind will lead to a change in actions, as Christ said, *"and do the first works."*

And the beautiful thing about repentance? We have a loving God who is inviting us to return, waiting for us to respond. I love this passage in Isaiah, which shows the heart of God:

"And therefore will the Lord wait, that He may be gracious unto you, and therefore will He be exalted, that He may have mercy upon you: for the Lord is a God of judgment: blessed are all they that wait for Him." 30:18)

Putting it into Practice

God is waiting for His children to turn. His desire is for that *"first love"* closeness of fellowship and relationship with us. How foolish we are to push Him away for the deceitful pleasures of sin! And yet, even so, He gives us this promise:

"Draw nigh to God, and He will draw nigh unto you. Cleanse your hands, ye sinners; and purify your hearts, ye double minded. Be afflicted, and mourn, and weep: let your laughter be turned to mourning, and your joy to heaviness. Humble yourselves in the sight of the Lord, and He shall lift you up." (James 4:8-10)

Repentance is not to be a flippant or superficial assent to

the truth of God, nor is it merely the making of resolutions or "turning over of a new leaf."

True repentance is a turning of heart and mind, a returning to the Lord in all the humility and gratitude and love—the "first love" of a soul saved through the blood of Christ.

In the depths of our humility and sorrow over how we have fallen, we mourn over how we have let our love for God cool, allowing sin and self to take Christ's place in our hearts and lives. But even so, we do not despair, for we have the hope of a loving God who desires to forgive and restore.

"The Lord is good unto them that wait for Him, to the soul that seeketh Him." Lamentations 3:25

*J.I. Packer, "Marks of Revival"

5

Results of Revival

"Surely His salvation is nigh them that fear Him; that glory may dwell in our land. Mercy and truth are met together; righteousness and peace have kissed each other. Truth shall spring out of the earth; and righteousness shall look down from heaven. Yea, the Lord shall give that which is good; and our land shall yield her increase. Righteousness shall go before Him; and shall set us in the way of His steps." (Psalm 85:9-13)

We tend to view revival as this elusive event, far off in the mists of history or past the horizons of the future. We look for revival in the future either with hopeful expectation, or the skepticism of discouragement. But we don't have to wait for a worldwide revival, or even a national or city-wide revival.

You don't even have to wait for revival to sweep through your local church to enjoy its results. For, as we have already seen, revival has to do with a heart hearing and responding in faith-fueled obedience to God. Large-scale revivals neverthe-less must take place heart-by-heart, Christian-by-Christian, one-by-one.

We have already looked at what revival is, and how it comes about, but now let's turn our focus to the results:

"Surely His salvation is nigh them that fear Him; that glory may dwell in our land. Mercy and truth are met together; right-eousness and peace have kissed each other. Truth shall spring out of the earth; and righteousness shall look down from heaven. Yea, the Lord shall give that which is good; and our land shall yield her increase. Righteousness shall go before Him; and shall set us in the way of His steps." (Psalm 85:9-13)

This idyllic picture describes life lived in right relationship to God. It is full of peace, joy, and beauty. It is characterized by mercy, truth, and righteousness. These are the fruits of revival.

His salvation is near and vibrant to the revived. It swells within them a proper awe and reverence for God, the Judge of all, who so mercifully pardoned. And that mercy and pardon are not just vague or abstract ideas: they have been personally experienced, and are soul-deep reasons for rejoicing.

If you were to study the songs written during those great revivals of old, you would notice that Christ's saving work was a common theme. Take, for example, these first two stanzas from the hymn, "Here is Love," by William Rees, often referred to as "the love song of the Welsh Revival:"

Here is love, vast as the ocean,
Lovingkindness as the flood;
When the Prince of Life, our Ransom,
Shed for us His precious blood
Who His love will not remember?
Who can cease to sing His praise?
He can never be forgotten
Throughout Heav'n's eternal days.

~

On the mount of crucifixion
Fountains opened deep and wide;
Through the floodgates of God's mercy
Flowed a vast and gracious tide.
Grace and love, like mighty rivers,
Poured incessant from above,
And heav'n's peace and perfect justice
Kissed a guilty world in love.

For the Christian, a revived relationship with God centers on what Christ has done. It goes beyond the intellectual concept that Christ died for all, and embraces the heart-thrilling truth that He died for *me.*

But here in Psalm 85, salvation from sin is not necessarily what the psalmist is referring to. The Hebrew word has the sense of liberty, or deliverance, even prosperity. I think Psalm 86 illustrates this point beautifully:

> *"Bow down Thine ear, O Lord, hear me: for I am poor and needy.*
>
> *Preserve my soul; for I am holy: O Thou my God, save Thy servant that trusteth in Thee.*
>
> *Be merciful unto me, O Lord: for I cry unto Thee daily.*
>
> *Rejoice the soul of Thy servant: for unto Thee, O Lord, do I lift up my soul.*
>
> *For Thou, Lord, art good, and ready to forgive; and plenteous in mercy unto all them that call upon Thee.*
>
> *Give ear, O Lord, unto my prayer; and attend to the voice of my supplications.*
>
> *In the day of my trouble I will call upon Thee: for Thou wilt answer me." (vv.1-7)*

The psalm goes on in a similar manner, but these verses give us a good picture of what is happening. The revived Christian lives in the presence of God with a heart in such closeness and surrender to God that sin is confessed and turned from immediately. And with our hearts right with God, we can boldly ask for help, leaning on the truth of His nature, fearing nothing.

Because of the blood of Christ, we can come before the throne of God, saying with the psalmist in all honesty, "*I am holy.*" 1 John 1:9 tells us how:

"If we confess our sins, He is faithful and just to forgive us our sins, and to cleanse us from all unrighteousness."

When Christ died, He took our sin on Himself and exchanged it for His righteousness *(2 Corinthians 5:21).* When we are right with God, all sin confessed and turned from, we can boldly enter the presence of the Lord *(Hebrews 4:16).*

A Christian harboring sin or neglecting God does not have this confidence. Rather, the goodness of God is a reminder of His justice, and His readiness to forgive is a reminder of the sin of which he or she is unwilling to let go.

Though still saved, a Christian in need of revival tends to have a distant or even negative view of God. In the darkness of a heart yielded to temptation rather than to God, Satan often plants a doubt that God is good, or even an idea that He is somehow malicious or overly stern.

This begins to seem possible for the Christian clinging to sin, because all they see is the justice side of God's character. By ignoring or pushing away the Holy Spirit's conviction, they are rejecting the very mercy of God calling them to enjoy His goodness.

Revival is the meeting of mercy and truth. Truth brings the consciousness of our sin as it truly is in the eyes of God. It humbles and convicts our hearts so that God can pour His mercy on us through forgiveness and restoration.

The revived Christian is a picture of Christ's mercy and truth, but also of His righteousness and peace. As we respond to the Holy Spirit's conviction of sin with true repentance, our lives begin to reflect the character of Christ.

Remember, revival is essentially a work of the Holy Spirit in the hearts of individuals. Notice the contrast between the works of the flesh and the fruit of the Spirit in these verses from the book of Galatians:

> *"Now the works of the flesh are manifest, which are these; Adultery, fornication, uncleanness, lasciviousness, Idolatry, witchcraft, hatred, variance, emulations, wrath, strife, seditions, heresies, Envyings, murders, drunkenness, revellings, and such like: of the which I tell you before, as I have also told you in time past, that they which do such things shall not inherit the kingdom of God.*
>
> *But the fruit of the Spirit is love, joy, peace, longsuffering, gentleness, goodness, faith, Meekness, temperance: against such there is no law."*
> *(5:19-23)*

Do you see what a difference the Holy Spirit makes? A large revival is not some mystical event, some magic convergence of just the right circumstances and societal conditions, but rather the contagiousness of Christ. It is the holy attraction of Christians walking in the Spirit, exhibiting the righteousness of Christ in the humility of a worshipful heart.

As we live close to God, the fruit of the Spirit replaces the works of the flesh, and two things happen: Christians see it and are convicted and encouraged to seek God themselves, and the unsaved see it and are brought face to face with mercy and truth. That is why revivals start with the saved, but often result in many unsaved coming to Christ.

When we are walking close to God, in obedience to the Holy Spirit, we choose blessing over judgement, and we can rest in the goodness of God, no matter what we encounter from day to day.

We can trust that the God who kept His promise that, *"whosoever shall call upon the name of the Lord shall be saved" (Romans 10:13),* is able and faithful also to keep the promise of Romans 8:28 *"all things work together for good to them that love God, to them who are the called according to His purpose."*

Revival results in a precious closeness with God, and since God's ways always work, revival points others to God.

Putting it into Practice

By this point in our study, dear Reader, my hope and prayer is that you are experiencing all the blessing and joyfulness of a heart revived to a new closeness with the Savior. But before we part, just one more word of advice: Christians are intended to live each day in the state of constant revival.

If you are enjoying revival in your relationship with God, stay close! It is a daily, moment by moment fight that requires diligence and attentiveness. But as always, your relationship with God is worth it!

May you and I embrace personal revival each day, walking in the Spirit today and every day!

"If we live in the Spirit, let us also walk in the Spirit."

Galatians 5:25

Learning Ladyhood Press

Devotional Commentaries
Wholesome Fiction
Hymns for the Heart Devotional Series

For more books by this author, visit Learning Ladyhood.com

www.ingramcontent.com/pod-product-compliance
Lightning Source LLC
Chambersburg PA
CBHW060357130626
46553CB00003B/1269